Blockchain: A Guide to Understanding Blockchain

I0481522

Book #3 of the book series by Cryptomasher

Sean Bennett

Intro Page

Congratulations on downloading *Blockchain: A Guide to Understanding Blockchain* and thank you for doing so. Blockchain technology is in the news more and more these days, especially as Bitcoin prices continue to climbs higher and higher. Generating plenty of news for speculative investors to obsess over is only one of its many uses, however, and it is likely going to be those who put it to use solving problems in new and creative ways that really win out once all the speculation has finished.

Each blockchain is a decentralized database which stores data in such a way that it allows for easy access by a wide variety of users while still offering top rate security and ease of use. It is for these reasons that many experts are already calling it the most significant new technological innovation since the creation of the internet despite the fact that less than 50 percent of the population can accurately describe what a blockchain is, and less than 10 percent interact with it on a regular basis.

This book will cover the following:

- The Fundamentals of Blockchain

- Smart Contracts

- The Story Behind Blockchain

- How Blockchain Works

- Main Participants in a Blockchain Transaction

- Key Elements in Block Batching & Stacking

It will not only cover this, but you will also learn about:

- Utilization of Blockchain and its Importance

- How Blockchain Can Improve Your Business

- Learning the Basics and History of Cryptocurrency
- The Future that Blockchain Holds
- How it Will Shape the Economy

Enjoy the third book in the series from Cryptomasher!

Once again thank you for purchasing the book and I hope you enjoy it.

Table of Contents

Introduction..6
Chapter 1: Blockchain Basics......................................8
Chapter 2: A Brief History Blockchain....................13
Chapter 3: A Look at How Blockchain Works.........16

    Proof of Work...19
    Proof of Stake...20

Chapter 4: Practical Applications of Blockchain.....23
Chapter 5: Blockchain and Your Business...............32

    Shared Ledger...32
    Permissions..33
    Consensus..34

Chapter 6: Understanding Cryptocurrency.............43
Chapter 7: Blockchain in the Future.......................54
Conclusion...61

Introduction

It is unlikely that you are completely unfamiliar with the concept of blockchain technology, you can certainly be forgiven for not having the clearest grasp on what exactly it is all about. Luckily, you are in good company as less than 50 percent of Americans can accurately describe the specifics surrounding blockchain technology and less than 10 percent interact with it on a regular basis.

While it is still relatively early days for the technology as a whole, blockchain technology promises to have far-reaching financial, economic and social implications across a wide variety of fields and industries. By utilizing a global peer-to-peer system to directly and transparently guarantee the integrity of transactions between parties, blockchain is already working to transform various vital industries that supply or depend on third-party verification. Never before has it been possible to pair easily verifiable transactions with an inalterable, error-proof ledger.

Despite having been around for less than a decade, it is already making great strides when it comes to improving the transparency and honesty in all forms of transactions, including in the battle against bribery, corruption and other fraudulent practices. It is also currently working on making extensive changes to the way supply chains are dealt with, and is also working at a governmental level, to change services including central banking. This book equips you with an understanding of what blockchain is, how it works, and how it can improve a business or industry. You will learn the essentials of blockchain and how this innovation will reform transactions and business frameworks. You will also discover what makes blockchain an ideal solution for business networks.

Blockchain continues to open new doors for businesses willing to invest in the technology and do business in a completely transparent way across the globe. Soon, blockchain may even become the standard ledger of every industry and sector. As such, in order to prepare yourself for the oncoming revolution you will find in the following chapters everything you need in order to understand blockchain technology and to put it to use in a profitable way.

Every effort was made to ensure it is full of as much useful information as possible.

Chapter 1: Blockchain Basics

What Is Covered In This Chapter?

The Fundamentals of Blockchain

Smart Contracts

Investors are increasingly using blockchain to generate higher amounts of revenue, and businesses both big and small are currently considering the ways they can use them to get ahead of the competition, however less than half the population can give an accurate definition of a blockchain and less than 10 percent interact with them directly on a regular basis.

While the use of the term can vary by context, the most important feature of all blockchains is their ability to store a wide variety of data, though it is primarily financial in nature these days, in a specialized database. You may find it helpful to think of the word blockchain like you would the word Lego, many different things can be made from Lego while all sharing a handful of important similarities and all existing under the same brand name. To wit, all blockchains are going to store data of some type and allow unparalleled access while providing near unbeatable security. Each block in a blockchain holds data related to the chain as a whole while also taking in new data which is then automatically replicated across the entire chain after it is verified. Thus we can define blockchain as *'a chain of growing successive unalterable blocks of data built upon one another.'*

What is Blockchain Technology?

Blockchain is a disseminated database of open records which document all transactions or advanced events that have been executed prior to that point which is shared among participating members. Every transaction in the public record is confirmed by agreement by a larger part of the members within that framework. Once entered, data can never be erased or altered. The blockchain contains a certain and evident record of each transaction made at any point in time.

The blockchain innovation is flawless and has worked impeccably over time. While general usage is still relatively scarce, it has already been successfully linked to both financial and logistical transactions. Marc Andreessen, the doyen of Silicon Valley's business visionaries, called the blockchain consensus model the most important invention since the internet itself. Johann Palychata from BNP Paribas stated in *Quintessence Magazine* that Bitcoin's blockchain - the backbone of the prominent cryptocurrency - ought to be viewed as a creation like the steam or combustion engine that has the ability to change the world of finance forever.

The current economy is based around an intricate web of trust. All our online transactions depend on trusting someone or something, both to ensure that our data gets where it needs to be and also to let us know when it has, in fact, reached its destination- it could be an email service provider disclosing that our emails have been sent; it could be a certification authority stating that a specific digital certificate is dependable; or it could be an online community like Facebook confirming that our posts have been shared with 'only' our friends.

In the most important case, it can be a bank disclosing that our cash has been delivered to a third party or that our deposits have gone through successfully. The truth of the matter is that we carry on with our lives by trusting third parties for the security and protection of our digital and non-digital resources. The reality remains, however, that these third-party sources can be compromised or hacked. It is here where the innovation of blockchain truly shines. It is a potential reformer of the digital world through its ability to enable a distributed consensus where every single transaction can be confirmed at any time by any party who was associated with the transaction. Furthermore, it does this without compromising the protection of the digital assets and parties involved. The distributed consensus and anonymity, are two essential qualities of the blockchain innovation.

Blocks

- Records in a blockchain are arranged in batches called blocks.
- The records within blocks cannot be altered.
- The blocks are a continuously growing list.
- Transactions are grouped in blocks every 10 minutes.
- Blocks of the past cannot be altered

In a blockchain, the records are arranged in batches called *blocks*. The records within these blocks cannot be altered. The blocks are a continuously growing list. Typically, the transactions are grouped in blocks of transactions every 10 minutes.

The blockchain database automatically updates itself as soon as any change happens.

The bitcoin network blocks of the past cannot be altered because that would mean any block following that block number would need to be regenerated. Such a functionality is not available and is never planned to be made available.

Node

Blockchain database is distributed across many peer-to-peer networks of computers. These individual systems are called nodes. Each node on the network will have a full copy of the entire transaction history from its inception till the current transaction. As time goes on, many more transactions will get added to the current blockchain, thereby unveiling a timeline of how the blockchain evolved. Nodes are thus computers that constantly run the blockchain software. Their function is to detect and validate new blocks.

For validating, updating, or retrieving any data, all the previous records can be easily obtained from the nodes. The validation done by the nodes occurs using something known algorithms. Whenever someone requests a transaction or alteration, it is broadcast to the network of nodes for verification. After the verification happens, the details of this transaction is encrypted and a new block is created for the ledger and added to the blockchain. The transaction is then deemed complete.

Hash

Each block identifies and references the previous block. This is done using something called a hash. It is a short, random sequence of letters and numbers.

Basically, every new block created after the original genesis block contains a hash of the previous network block. Each new block can be generated only in a chronological order since it contains the hash of a previous block. If not, the hash would be shown as unknown and the network will reject the block.

Ease of verification

Using the blockchain technology, the participants (sender and receiver) can transfer the assets without needing any centralized third-party verification. The decentralized nature of blockchain also gives it a major advantage, as it means there is no central point of failure that can bring down blockchain.

Unspent Transaction Outputs cache (UTXO)

The additional database kept by the nodes is called as UTXO. This is a ledger which works as a cache for the blockchain. UXTO consists of the record of funds available for each and every address. It is updated whenever there is a new transaction and funds get debited from the sending address and gets added to the receiving address.

Smart Contracts

One key use of blockchain includes smart contracts. Smart contracts are essentially bite-sized computer programs that activate at specified points based on external events. When pre-designed conditions in a smart contract are met, the next term of agreement associated with that contract is activated until all terms have been met. All of that information is recorded in the blockchain and is available in a completely trusted and transparent way. You can think of a smart contract as operating in much the same way a vending machine. Specifically, when a consumer inserts currency into a vending machine, they must enter a value to select an item. Once an item is selected, the item then drops down and the consumer is able to collect their item. In a smart contract all of these actions are executed automatically based on external factors and recorded in a blockchain.

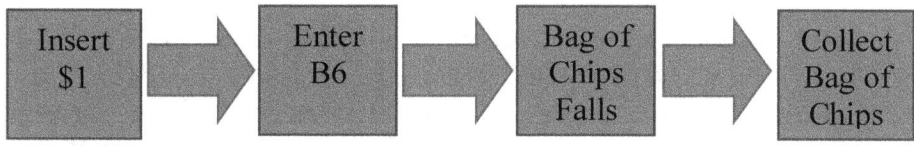

Insert $1 → Enter B6 → Bag of Chips Falls → Collect Bag of Chips

Blockchain technology is already taking off as a serious driver of digital innovation. Blockchain through the use of smart contracts is the next step in the recording and execution of terms. It makes perfect business sense to use this technology for complete trust and transparency of information.

Chapter 2: A Brief History Blockchain

What Is Covered In This Chapter?

The Story Behind Blockchain

The history of blockchain and the history of Bitcoin are directly intertwined. When its distributed ledger was initially developed in 2009, digital money was considered an impossibility due to the relative simplicity of duplicating digital data. This is otherwise called the "double-spend" issue where every transaction held the risk of the original owner spending the same currency twice before the first transaction could be successfully verified.

The traditional method for alleviating this risk had been to use a trusted third party, for example, a bank, acting as a central body to monitor such transactions. The creator of Bitcoin removed this obligation by creating an entire system for blockchain that is in charge of handling this verification process. Transactions that take place on the blockchain are typically verified using what is known as a proof of work system which requires that those verifying the transaction, generally known as miners, solve a complicated mathematical formula to ensure the transaction is legitimate.

Blockchain Iterations

While having only been in existence for less than a decade, blockchain technology has already seen a vast number of improvements. Each wave of improvements has included a new designation - blockchain 1.0 and 2.0. The class "blockchain 1.0" contains early cryptocurrencies, for example, Bitcoin, that can be utilized as an alternative option to more traditional monetary forms (e.g. the euro or dollar). Right up until today, Bitcoin continues to be the blockchain application best known to the world. However, in spite of the way that an ever-increasing number of clients are embracing the currency, with transaction volumes ever on the rise, the outright number of Bitcoin transactions in the global remote trade markets is still quite small, though there are signs that this is changing.

The second phase of advancement came along with the introduction of smart contract models. A smart contract represents a computerized protocol that automatically executes predefined procedures of a contract without requiring the inclusion of an outsider (e.g. a bank). For instance, it would be possible to make a completely automated smart contract between an energy producer and a buyer that self-governs and safely controls both supply and payment. On the off chance that the client was to neglect to make payment, the smart contract would automatically mastermind the power supply to be suspended until the point when payment has been received, given the parties involved had beforehand consented to incorporate such a system in their agreement. This improvement represents a risk to the customary plans of action of banks, which might be in peril of being rejected from the market section of payments.

Private Versus Public Blockchains

Organizations and designers may choose to construct their applications on either private or public blockchains. In private blockchain frameworks, all members are known and recognized before being given access. On a public blockchain, the personality of all members stays anonymous. Bitcoin and Ethereum are the most well-known examples of a public blockchain.

A few favorable aspects of private blockchains are that they are considerably less complex than their public counterparts which means they will cost far less to create, and maintain, especially as the blockchain members can verify transactions which means payment for third party verification does not to be

factored into the costs. As such, numerous different banks and payment service providers, including JP Morgan, are currently looking into ways to utilize private blockchains for their current plans of action.

Chapter 3: A Closer Look at How Blockchain Works

What Is Covered In This Chapter?

How Blockchain Works and Why it Matters

Blockchain owes its name to the way it stores transactional information — in blocks that are connected together to form a chain. As the quantity of transactions increase, so does the size of the blockchain as a whole. Blocks record and verify the time and arrangement of transactions, which are then verified before being added to the blockchain as a whole. The blocks are governed by generally agreed rules which are developed at the time of the blockchain's creation.

Hashing

Each block contains a hash (a unique identifier or digital fingerprint), a batch of timestamped recent genuine transactions along with the hash of the previous block stored on a node. The previous block's hash connects the blocks together and keeps any block from being changed or a block being embedded between two existing blocks. Therefore, each resulting block fortifies the identity of the previous block and consequently the whole blockchain. Essentially, every hash is recorded on every block every single time making it impossible to remove a block. If a block is removed it would become immediately evident that the blockchain has been tampered with. This strategy of recording information makes the blockchain ultra-clear, contributing to the key characteristic of its unchanging nature.

Note: While the blockchain does contains transactional information, it is not a substitute for transaction processing, messaging technology or business forms. The blockchain only contains a confirmed 'proof' of transactions. Nonetheless, while blockchain basically works as a database for recording transactions, its advantages reach out far past those of a conventional database.

Main Participants in a Blockchain Transaction

Different members on a blockchain system assume a part in its operation. The following are depictions of each of the members:

- **Blockchain client**: A member (generally a business client) with authorizations to join the blockchain system and create transactions with other system members. Blockchain innovation works out of sight, so the blockchain client has no awareness of it. There are normally various clients on any one business system.

- **Regulator**: A blockchain client with higher than average authority when it comes to directing the transactions occurring inside the system. Regulators are only found in private blockchains.

- **Blockchain developer**: Programmers who make the applications and smart contracts that empower blockchain clients to creating transactions on the blockchain. Applications work as a conduit between clients and the blockchain.

- **Blockchain network administrator**: Individuals who have special authority and permission to define, create, oversee, and monitor the blockchain system. Every business on a private blockchain will have a blockchain system administrator.

- **Traditional processing platforms**: Existing computer frameworks that might be utilized by the blockchain to increase processing. This framework may likewise need to initiate demands of the blockchain.

- **Traditional information sources**: Existing information frameworks that may give information to impact the conduct of smart contracts and help to characterize how interchanges and information exchanges will happen between customary applications/information and the blockchain — by means of API calls, through MQ style cloud messaging, or both.

- **Certificate specialist**: An individual who issues and deals with the diverse sorts of certificates required to run a permissioned, private, blockchain. For instance, certificates may need be issued to blockchain clients or for individual transactions.

Key Elements in Block Batching & Stacking

- **Transaction definition**: The "Sender" makes a transaction and transmits it to the system. The transaction message incorporates subtle elements of the Receiver's public address, the estimation of the transaction, and a cryptographic digital signature that demonstrates the legitimacy of the transaction.

- **Transaction verification**: The nodes (PCs/clients) of the system get the message and verify its legitimacy by unscrambling the digital signature. The verified transaction is put in a pool of pending transactions.

- **Block creation**: These pending transactions are assembled in an updated version of the ledger, called a block, by one of the nodes in the system. At a particular time, the node communicates the block to the system for approval.

- **Block validation**: Each other node in the system get the proposed block and work to approve it through an iterative procedure which requires agreement from a greater part of the system, specifically 51 percent of all active nodes need to confirm the new block in order for it to be added to the blockchain. Different blockchain systems utilize different means of verification. Bitcoin's blockchain utilizes a system called "proof of work", Ripple utilizes "Distributed Consensus", and Ethereum will soon be switching to a "proof of stake" model. The different methods have distinctive upsides and downsides. However, they all guarantee that each transaction is substantial, and they make false transactions very unlikely.

- **Block chaining**: If all transactions are approved, the new block is "chained" into the blockchain, and the new current condition of the ledger is communicated to the system. This entire procedure can be finished in 3-10 seconds.

Proof of Work and Proof of Stake Concepts

The motivation behind the verification process is to accomplish agreement on the contents of the distributed ledger. Agreement-based checks are (1) decentralized (i.e. inserted on the blockchain itself) and (2) automated process. These two instruments are most generally used to build up agreement which are then inserted into the blockchain.

Proof of Work

The proof of work idea is the agreement system most often utilized in public blockchains, and depends on third parties known as miners. Each block is confirmed through mining before its data is added to the chain. The information contained in each block is checked using algorithms which connect a distinct hash to each piece of information depending on the data stored in it.

In order to verify transactions, miners utilize specialized mining machines which are powerful computers designed to solve the equations that come along with a proof of work model as quickly as possible. The level of difficulty required to verify a transaction often adjusts as a response to the miners' network's computing power. This happens in order to guarantee that new blocks can be hashed at predefined intervals (Bitcoin: 10 minutes, Ethereum: 10 seconds) regardless of the possibility that only a single piece of data relating to any transaction is eventually changed.

For instance, if a transaction is modified because of tampering or because of transmission blunders, the algorithm associated with the block will never again deliver the right hash and its related block will never make it into the blockchain. The hashes processed for a similar block, which was stored around the decentralized system are compared so that changed blocks can be recognized and pronounced as invalid. Once the block which contains the underlying transaction is added to the blockchain, the transaction is confirmed to the two participants. Decisions made as per the proof of work standard are adopted on the premise of the measure of work the individual partners have performed to confirm a block.

Proof of Stake

The proof of stake concept eases the mining procedure where a large number of transactions need to be verified. While under the proof of work standard, a huge number of distributed miners are consistently verifying the hashes of transactions through the mining procedure so as to update the current status of the blockchain, the proof of stake idea expects clients to repeatedly demonstrate responsibility for a claim share ("stake") in the basic currency.

Where the proof of stake technique is utilized, the work required to do the confirmation procedure is allocated between the members depending on their percentage stake. For instance, if a client possesses a 10% portion of the aggregate blockchain resources, the client should do 10% of the required mining work. This approach considerably decreases the complex quality of the decentralized confirmation process and would thus be able to deliver huge savings on working expenses and energy.

While there are no blockchains that are currently utilizing this type of verification process, the Ethereum platform is currently taking strides to implement the first phase of a plan to switch to this type of verification model sometime in early 2018. Using what is being called as the Casper Proof of Stake model, it will start by taking one block out of every 100 and verifying it using a proof of stake model as described above. In the Beta stages of proof of stake this process with then be double-checked using the standard proof of work model to verify its efficacy.

The goal of this type of verification model is to improve the rates at which new blocks are created as there will no longer be a lengthy period where miners are forced to complete a complicated proof of work model that is only going to get more complicated as time goes on and more and more transactions are added to the blockchain.

When this system is put into effect it will mark the first time a non-proof of work model has been used in any blockchain which has the potential to open up the possibilities for what verification can entail significantly. It will also serve as the first live test of the proof of stake model in any form which will allow the blockchain community as a whole to determine if there is something more effective out there than the standard proof of work model. This is particularly relevant as it only requires a fraction of the energy that a proof of work verification does. This would be a serious boon to heavily trafficked blockchains such as Bitcoin which spend enough verifying each transaction to power an average sized home for a week. For reference, there are about 300,000 bitcoin transactions per day.

Chapter 4: Practical Applications of Blockchain

Below are some practical applications of Blockchain which can help in financial and non-financial business use.

Financial Applications

The money related services industry has several noteworthy use cases for blockchain, starting with business financing.

Organizations need to buy products and services using a credit card with end-to-end visibility to avoid and resolve transaction issues. The advantages of including complete visibility of the order-to-delivery channel include decreasing the number of issues documented, as well as the time required to sort out any relevant issues.

Trade Applications

Organizations require an approach to streamline the way of getting endorsements from different legal agencies (customs, port authorities, trucking or rail transportation firms, et cetera) for any cross-border movement. Here is another place that blockchain technology shines as it can be utilized by these agencies to sign all the relevant paperwork, and it keeps all parties in the loop with respect to the status of the product in question, when products are received and when payment is transferred from the buyer to the seller.

The advantages for this includes the following:

- Complex processes combined into a single effective process, all thanks to access to a distributed ledger
- Increased access to capital, since it is not held up in long settlement times or because of mistakes and issues
- Increased trust, accountability and responsibility among all parties across all transactions.

Cross-Border Transactions

Banks require an approach to oversee nostro/vostro accounts. Nostro (our own) alludes to a record a residential bank holds in a remote bank in the foreign nation's currency. Vostro (yours) is the way the remote bank refers to that record. Such accounts are utilized to encourage and disentangle a transaction and foreign transactions through compromise. Nostro/vostro records can move toward becoming recorded transactions on a blockchain to significantly enhance transparency and productivity through a computerized compiled set of records.

The advantages include:

- The capacity to oversee transactions on all of a bank's vostro/nostro accounts through a single interface
- Greater visibility of transaction statuses, current balances, and tracking of the aforementioned
- Consistent, timely, and precise picture over all nostro/vostro accounts

Insurance

The insurance business can also utilize blockchain in numerous time-saving ways. Insurance suppliers require a proficient approach to process claims, confirm that an insurable event really happened, and furnish clients with reasonable and timely payouts. With self-governing protection

claims processing, policy conditions are built into a smart contract stored on the blockchain and associated with openly accessible information by means of the Internet. At whatever point an accident occurs and is accounted for by a trusted source, such as an internet enabled vehicle, the smart contract is triggered, and the claim is handled by the terms of the arrangement indicated in the smart contract, and, if applicable, the client is paid without having to wait for an actual claims adjuster to get involved.

The advantages for insurance are as follows:

- Eliminates the cost of preparing insurance claims
- Reduces the chance for insurance fraud
- Improves consumer loyalty

Government

A lot of government red tape stems from the need to record transactions and where they came from. As such, many longstanding processes can take advantage of blockchain's benefits to become more productive and straightforward.

Setting up trusted identities remains an ongoing issue for governments because of forgery and the high cost typically associated with confirming this information. As a result, millions of people, most of those children, go undocumented and unidentified each year. Individuals in the poorer parts of the world might not have adequate confirmation to build up an identity as required by certain organizations; for instance, banks commonly require evidence of home or service bills to set up identity, neither of which may exist in developing nations.

Organizations can make use of blockchain technology by issuing digitally certified birth certificates that are unforgeable, time-stamped, and open to any authorized body on the planet.

The advantages of this include:

- Reduced expenses and time in checking identities
- Reduction in human trafficking
- Transparency in grant designations

Supply Chain Management

When something turns out badly with a complex "network of networks", for example, when an airplane crashes, it is essential to know the quality of every piece of that plane from the most complex part, down to the simplest screw. Blockchain technology can make this process much more manageable through inventory network administration, and easily allow you to find the details on every segment, down to the producer, generation date, cluster, and even the assembling machine.

Advantages include:

- Increased trust on the grounds that no single authority "claims" the provenance data
- Increased efficiencies prompt decreases in time taken to analyze and cure a fault, enhancing framework usage
- Specific reviews as opposed to non-specific
- Source origin is likewise essential in the sustenance production network.

Healthcare

The healthcare industry needs a more proficient and secure framework for overseeing medical records, settling insurance claims, pre-authorizing payments, and performing and recording other complex transactions. Blockchain guarantees this necessary help. Blockchain can improve these muddled and tedious processes and automate the accumulation and sharing of data.

Extra advantages can include:

- Claims can be checked on and paid all the more effectively and rapidly.
- The framework can recommend alternative services with better coverage.
- Gradual reduction of waste and eventual cost saving

Non-Financial Applications

A number of financial uses were covered above. In this section some non-financial applications will be presented.

Electronic Medical Records

Electronic medical records are at present kept on servers either within the facility or within the cloud, and access is constrained to hospital facility and care provider systems. Centralization of such data makes it a much easier target for digital theft. On the other hand, a blockchain can easily hold the total medical history for every patient, with numerous granularities of control by the patient, specialists, doctors, administrators, regulators, hospitals, insurers, etc., giving a protected framework to record and keep up an exhaustive medical history for each patient. In fact, these systems are already being tested in real-world settings and the results are impressive. These tests show that patients are 40 percent less likely to have their files mismanaged with the blockchain system than without, especially in emergency situations.

The following are other advantages:

- Tamper-safe methods for securing medical history
- Reduced time in determination of insurance claims
- Complete medical history of the patient for use by doctors for recommendation of exact medication

Notary Public

Confirming credibility of a transaction can be possible utilizing blockchain and removes the requirement for a central authority who can take responsibility for verifying the transaction. The record verification helps in authenticating the Proof of Ownership (who authored it), Proof of Existence (at what specific time) and Proof of Integrity (not altered) of the reports. Since it can be checked by independent intermediaries, these services can serve as a stand in during situations that would traditionally call for a notary.

Utilizing a blockchain for notarization secures the privacy of the record and the identity of any individuals who look for confirmation. By making proof of publication available to relevant parties, the blockchain takes the notary timestamping to new level. It additionally takes out the requirement for costly notarization charges and ineffectual methods for exchanging archives. Stampery, Block Notary, Crypto Public Notary, Proof of Existence, and Ascribe are examples of such organizations

The Music Industry

The music business has undergone several major changes since the start of the twenty-first century. It is affecting everybody in the music business - artists, publishers, labels, distributors, lyricists and streaming service providers. The procedure by which music royalties are determined has dependably been a convoluted one, yet the ascent of the Internet has influenced it significantly leading to a desire for more transparency from all sides.

Blockchain technology will come into play to solve these challenges as it makes keeping up an extensive, precise disseminated database of music rights ownership data much more manageable by placing it in a public ledger. The royalty split for each work, as dictated by smart contracts could be added to the database, in addition to rights ownership information. The smart contracts would characterize connections between various partners (addresses) and automate their collaborations.

Decentralized Proof of Existence Documents

Approving the existence or the ownership of signed documents is imperative in any legitimate arrangement. The traditional document approval models depend on central bodies for storing and approving the documents, which display some conspicuous security challenges. These models turn out to be more troublesome as the reports becomes older.
The blockchain innovation gives an option model to proof-of-existence and ownership of authoritative records.

By utilizing the blockchain, a client can just store the signature and timestamp related with a legitimate record in the blockchain and approve it whenever utilizing native blockchain mechanisms. The main benefit of this service is privacy and protection that enables a client to give decentralized verification of the document that cannot be changed by an outsider. The existence of the record is approved utilizing blockchain that does not rely upon a single centralized element.

Decentralized Storage

Cloud file storage solutions, for example, Google Drive, One Drive, or Dropbox, are an increasingly popular way to store files, photographs, video and music. Despite their prevalence, cloud document storage solutions ordinarily confront challenges in areas like data control, privacy, and security. The significant issue is that one has to trust a third party with one's private documents.

Storage service providers can use a blockchain based peer-to-peer distributed cloud storage platform that enables clients to exchange and offer information without depending on an outside information supplier. This enables individuals to share unused web data transfer capacity and extra hard drive space in their PCs and laptops with those in need of extra space in return for bitcoin based microtransactions.

Decentralized IoT

The Internet of Things (IoT) is progressively becoming a popular innovation in both the business and the consumer space. Most IoT platforms depend on a concentrated model in which a node or agent controls the communication between devices. However, this approach has turned out to be illogical for some situations in which devices need to trade information between themselves autonomously. This particular prerequisite has prompted endeavors towards decentralized IoT platforms which is where blockchain technology comes into play.

The blockchain innovation encourages the usage of decentralized IoT platforms, in secured and trusted information exchanges and also record keeping. In such a design, the blockchain works as the general record, keeping a trusted record of the considerable number of messages traded between smart devices in a decentralized IoT topology.

Blockchain Based Anti-Counterfeit Solutions

Forgery and counterfeiting are some of the greatest challenges facing the present-day economy. Existing solutions depend on an inherent level of trust from an intermediary that presents a sensible balance to those on both sides of a transaction. Blockchain makes these traditional services unnecessary thanks to its decentralized ledger format coupled with its extremely tight security. One can imagine a situation, in which brands, shippers and commercial centers are all just pieces of a blockchain network with nodes storing data to approve the validity of various products. With the utilization of this innovation, partners in the supply chain do not require dependence on a centralized authority for credibility of the branded items.

Chapter 5: Blockchain and Your Business

What Is Covered In This Chapter?

How Blockchain Can Improve Your Business

Blockchain has many uses which have been demonstrated above along with the key players and parts of a blockchain. While currently only the standard proof of work system of blockchain exists the concept of the proof of stake can become a viable alternative to the current standard. Now how does all of this apply to you as an individual or a business owner? The following chapter will elucidate this.

What Makes a Blockchain Suitable for Business?

Rather than having a blockchain that depends on the trading of digital forms of money with unknown clients on an open system (similar to the case with bitcoin), a blockchain for business is a private, permissioned system that has the ability to perform many of the functions of a more traditional database.

To have a better understanding of how a blockchain for business functions, and to value its potential for reforming business systems, you have to comprehend the following key ideas of blockchain for business.

Shared Ledger

The ledger functionality of a blockchain is nothing different to what has been utilized as a part of double-entry accounting system since the thirteenth century. What it does bring to the equation, however, is the idea of a common, distributed ledger

– a changeless record of all transactions on the system, a record that all system members can get to. Transactions are recorded just once with a shared ledger, taking out the duplication of effort that is normal in conventional business systems.

The shared ledger has the following attributes:

- Records all transactions for both sides of the transaction with no additional effort
- Is shared among all members in the system
- Is permissioned, so members see just those transactions they are approved to see.

Permissions

Blockchains can either be permissioned or non-permissioned. With a permissioned blockchain, every member has a distinct identity, which allows the utilization of approaches to a constrained interest network and access to transaction information. With the capacity to constrain system membership, companies would be able to effortlessly conform to information security policies, for example, those stipulated in the Health Insurance Portability and Accountability Act (HIPAA). Additionally, permissioned blockchains are more efficient when it comes to controlling the consistency of the information that gets attached to a blockchain.

With the capacity to confine user access to relevant transactions, more involved transaction detail can be added to the blockchain without fear of that information ending up in the wrong people's hands. Furthermore, members can determine the transaction data they are willing to enable others to see. Additionally, a few members might be approved to see certain transactions, while others, for example, reviewers and auditors, might be offered access to a more extensive range of transactions. (With an open blockchain, the level of transaction detail might be constrained to ensure secrecy and obscurity.)

Consensus

In a business scenario where members are known and trusted, transactions can be verified and added to the blockchain in several different ways:

- **Proof of stake:** To approve transactions, validators must hold a specific level of the system's aggregate value. Proof of stake may give expanded assurance from a malicious attack on the system by decreasing incentives for attack by making it exceptionally costly to execute.
- **Multi-signature:** A dominant percentage of validators (for instance, three out of five) must concur that a transaction is legitimate.
- **Practical Byzantine Fault Tolerance (PBFT):** An algorithm intended to settle issues among computing nodes (network members) when one node in an arrangement of nodes creates a distinctive yield from the others in the set.

Advantages for Business

Blockchain can have the following specific advantages for businesses:

- **Time investment funds:** Transaction times for complex, multi-party collaborations are cut from days to minutes. Transaction payments are faster, in light of the fact that they are authenticated by members in a matter of seconds.

- **Cost savings***:* A blockchain system decreases costs in a few ways:

- Less oversight is required since the system is self-policed by system members, every one of whom are known on the system.
- Intermediaries are decreased since members can find all the details on transactions that concern them directly.
- Duplication of effort is wiped out since all members can access the shared ledger.

- **Tighter security:** Blockchain's security features protects against tampering, fraud, misrepresentation, and cybercrime. In the event that a system is permissioned, it empowers the formation of a participant-only system with evidence that participants are who they say they are and that ledger results are sure to be accurate.

- **Enhanced privacy:** Through the utilization of IDs and authorizations, clients can determine which transaction details they want other members to be permissioned to see. Authorizations can be extended for special users, for example, auditors, who may require access to more transaction information.

- **Improved auditability:** Having a shared ledger that serves as a solitary source of genuine information enhances the capacity to screen and review transactions.

- **Increased operational effectiveness:** Pure digitization of assets ensures that information required in order for business to flow smoothly is always contained in one place, and with smart contracts much of the back and forth required can be automated so items can be tracked, digitally signed for and paid for, all using smart contracts.

Building Trust with Blockchain

Blockchain encourages trust within a business relationship. It is not so much that you cannot believe the individuals who you are doing business with; it is that you do not have to worry about trust issues while working on a blockchain system.
Blockchain is especially profitable at expanding the level of trust among network members. Since each transaction builds on every other transaction, any attempt at modifying the chain is immediately clear. This self-policing can relieve the need to rely upon the currently accepted level of legitimate or government safe-guards and controls to screen and monitor the stream of business transactions. Instead, this is all taken care by members of the blockchain community.

Where outsider oversight is required, blockchain decreases the weight on the administrative framework by making it simpler for inspectors and regulators to audit significant transaction information and confirm compliance.

The following attributes are utilized by blockchain in building trust:

- **Distributed and manageable:** The record is shared, refreshed with each transaction, and specifically imitated among members. Since it is not possessed or controlled by any single association, the blockchain platform's continued presence is not reliant on any individual element.

- **Secure, private, and permanent:** Permissions and cryptography forestall unapproved access to the system and guarantee that members are who they claim to be. Security is managed through cryptographic systems as well as information partitioning strategies to give selective visibility to members in the system. After conditions are approved of, members cannot alter existing transactions; mistakes can be turned around only with new transactions.

- **Transparent and auditable:** Due members in a transaction have access to the same records, they can approve transactions and check identities or proprietorship without the requirement of middlemen. Transactions are time-stamped and can be easily verified after the fact.

- **Orchestrated and adaptable:** Because business principles and smart contracts can be incorporated into the platform, blockchain business systems can develop as they mature to help end-to-end business forms and an extensive variety of activities.

Risks for Adoption of Blockchain

Blockchain is a promising, innovative technology. As described earlier, there are a huge range of uses or issues that can be solved utilizing blockchain based innovation which range from financial to non-financial applications. A majority of these are radical developments. As it occurs with appropriation with radical developments, there are also risks of adoption.

Behavior change: Although change is constant, there is always going to be resistance to a serious change in the status quo. In the realm of a non-substantial trusted third party, that blockchain presents, clients need to get used to the idea that their transactions are safe, complete, and secured. The present day third parties like Visa or Mastercard (in case of a credit card) will likewise experience changed roles and obligations. As demand for these services increase, it is like that they will likewise contribute and move to block-based functionality. They will keep on providing the client relationship sort of services.

Scaling: Scaling of the current blockchain-based nascent services presents a challenge. Envision yourself executing a private blockchain transaction for the first time. In order to do so, you would need to download the whole system of existing transactions that make up the blockchain before executing your first transaction. This may take hours or longer as the quantity of blocks exponentially increase. This is a barrier to entry that is going to need to be addressed before blockchain technology can catch on in the mainstream.

Bootstrapping: Moving the current contracts or business archives/structures to the new blockchain based system introduces a critical system of movement assignments that will need to be approached properly in order for the transition to go smoothly. For instance, if there should be an occurrence of Real Estate proprietorships/liens, the current archives lying in County or Escrow organizations has to be moved to the identical blockchain form. This will involve time and cost.

Quantum Computing: The premise of blockchain innovation depends on the idea that the computing power required to trick a blockchain into thinking a block is false would far outweigh the potential gain. With the coming of quantum computers (in future), this may no longer be the case. The cryptographic keys might be sufficiently simple to break through by a sheer brute force approach within a short span of time.

Despite its challenges the scope and advantages of Blockchain technology far outweigh its perceived challenges.

Stages to Your First blockchain Application

After finding out the potentially transformative capacity of blockchain for business, you are likely anxious to discover what steps you have to take toward applying it in your business.

Below are the stages for your first blockchain application.

- **Decide whether blockchain has a place in your industry:** As you discover more about blockchain, you may find how it is now affecting your industry, or certain uses of blockchain may appear glaringly evident to you as answers to current difficulties. If you are unsure of whether blockchain has a place in your industry, ask yourself the following questions:

- Does my business system need to oversee legally binding contracts?
- Do we have to track transactions that include more than two participants?
- Is the present framework excessively complex or overpriced, probably because of the requirement for third parties or an essential issue of control?
- Can the system benefit from expanded trust, accountability, and transparency in recordkeeping?
- Is the present framework inclined to mistakes because of manual procedures or duplication of effort?
- Is the present exchange framework powerless against extortion, human error, and digital attack?

If your response to any of these inquiries is "yes", there is every likelihood of blockchain benefiting your industry.

- **Identify speed bumps in business processes:** Look at your present business processes for ineffectiveness, especially ventures in the process that are prone to delays, disappointment, blunders, and duplication of efforts. The questions in the previous segment are probably going to point you the correct way.
  A broader thing to ask may be: "What challenges do I confront in my exchange systems at the moment?"

- **Decide how blockchain can help:** After identifying the challenges in your transaction system, consider different properties of blockchain that can address the inefficiencies, costs, and other issues. For instance, if an absence of trust is an issue, blockchain's shared ledger can give extended visibility into transaction and asset details to enhance trust. On the off chance that business contracts or guidelines cause delays, smart contracts might be the answer. The objective here is to decide how blockchain can help conquer particular difficulties.

- **Select an appropriate use case:** While selecting a use case, ensure it is a match for what you are attempting to achieve. It has to be something that adds genuine value to your process, rather than something that could be accomplished similarly using the infrastructure you have in place. To determine if your use case is valid, ask the following questions:
    - Consensus: Does generating instantaneous consensus across the database add value?
    - Provenance: Is the upkeep of an entire review trail critical?
    - Immutability: Is it critical that the process of transaction is alter-proof?
    - Finality: Is there a requirement for a generally accepted "system of record" in the business framework?

- **Decide the goal of your blockchain network:** After picking a suitable use case, lay out a reasonable and measurable objective for your first undertaking.
    - What do you want to unravel or enhance using blockchain technology?
    - What would you be able to use to measure the level of achievement of your first venture in meeting that objective? Would you like to decrease resolution times? Accelerate claims processing? Free up capital stream? Lessen fraud in your system?

These are only a few conceivable goals a blockchain system could help accomplish.

- **Identify dependencies:** When you have a suitable use case at the top of the priority list, consider what else you require, in addition to the internal assets you currently have, to begin on your first blockchain venture. Do you require an administrative partner to help carry out the main venture? Do you require a platform that empowers you to meet certain compliance or administrative goals? Since exchange handling is turning into a group activity, a blockchain system is best when numerous participants are included and becomes even significantly more profitable and proficient as the blockchain develops.

- **Choose a blockchain provider and platform:** Pick a provider and platform that are the best fit for your business needs. In choosing the suitability of various providers and platforms, ask yourself the following questions:
    - Do you need a permissioned network?
    - Do you have to know the characters in your business network? For instance, to adhere to rules like know your client (KYC) or anti-money laundering (AML)?
    - Do you have frequent transactions with others that could be pre-programmed and automated, allowing for profitable time and resource?
    - Would you gain from transaction resolution in minutes as opposed to days or weeks?

- **Make a decision about moving forward:** Once you have all of the available data on blockchain technology and how it would benefit your business, the final step is to determine if it is the right choice for you and your company. While it can be easy to get caught up in wanting to adapt to the next big thing, this does not mean that switching to blockchain functionality is the right choice right now. If, after looking at the numbers, the functionality that blockchain technology would provide you with right now, does not make sense, it is important to look at the numbers rationally and move forward in stride rather than trying to force things to go in a more blockchain-focused direction. At the very least, you will have plenty of preliminary data the next time you feel it might be the right time, to switch to blockchain.

Chapter 6: Understanding Cryptocurrency

Learning the Basics and History of Cryptocurrency

The blockchain revolution grew out of the cryptocurrency network. Its inception and adoption is linked directly with what Bitcoin and other cryptocurrencies offered to the world. Below is a brief look at two of the most popular cryptocurrencies currently dominating the cryptomarket.

The Inadequacies of Current Transaction Frameworks

All throughout history, instruments of trust, for example, paper money, minted coins, letters of credit, and financial institutions, have risen to encourage the trading of value between buyers and sellers. Essential advancements, including phone lines, credit card frameworks, mobile technologies, and the internet have enhanced the comfort, speed, and effectiveness of transactions while at the same time reducing, and at times removing, the relative distance between buyers and sellers.

In any case, numerous business transactions remain wasteful, costly, and vulnerable, experiencing the following impediments:

- Cash is helpful just in local transactions and generally in small sums.
- There can be a long time between transactions and settlements.
- Duplication of effort and the requirement for a third-party approval add to the inefficiencies.

- Cyberattacks, fraud, and even simple slip-ups add to the cost and complexity of working together, and they expose all members in the system to risk if a central framework (for example, a bank) is breached.
- Credit card companies have basically made walled gardens with a high cost of entry. Vendors must pay the high expenses of onboarding, which regularly includes impressive printed material and a tedious confirming procedure.
- Half of the world's population do not have a bank account and have needed to create parallel payment frameworks to do transactions.

Worldwide, transaction volumes are developing exponentially and will unquestionably lead to additional complexities, inefficiencies, vulnerabilities, and expenses of current transaction frameworks. The development of online business, online banking, and in-application purchases, along with the rise in mobility of individuals around the globe have energized the increase in transaction volumes.

To address these difficulties and others, the world needs payment systems that are quick and that has a structure that builds up trust, requires no specific tools, has no transaction fees, and gives an aggregate account for guaranteeing transparency and trust.

The History of Cryptocurrency

What follows is a brief history of electronic money in all its forms:

Fiat Money and e-Money: The European Central Bank (ECB) defines fiat money as any legal tender assigned and issued by a central authority that individuals will acknowledge in return for goods and services since it is backed by regulations, and because they trust in this central authority. Fiat money is like commodity-backed money in when it comes to the ways it can be used, it differs however in that it cannot be exchanged directly for a commodity, for example, gold has to go through a third party to complete such a transaction. The most well-known type of fiat money backing is at the sovereign state's administration level, yet there have likewise been localized monetary forms or private monies.

The U.K. regulator defined Electronic money (e-money) as an electronically (including magnetically) stored monetary value, represented by a claim on the guarantor, which is issued on receipt of assets with the end goal of making payment transactions, and which is acknowledged by an individual other than the electronic money issuer. Forms of e-money include prepaid cards and electronic prepaid accounts for online utilization." Normally, e-money is stored in the same account unit as the fiat denomination that was used to procure it.

Cryptographically secure e-money: David Chaum was the first to put forth the idea of electronic money in the 1980s, his version required a token of cash that would copy physical money, and above all, allow for anonymous transactions. He based his fledgling cryptocurrency on an RSA encryption convention utilized for most security purposes, which prompted the establishment of the organization DigiCash. Because of inconveniences that emerged with the national bank in Amsterdam where DigiCash was established, it was decided that such money would just be sold as an item to banks. While it had a fair amount of baking at the time, it was not enough to cause it to stick around in the long-term.

After DigiCash, there was an explosion of small funding firms created to develop e-money frameworks, prompting the arrival of a key introductory administrative response to such e-money such as the 1994 EU Report by the Working Group on EU Payment Systems, which was made to the council of the European Monetary Institute. After the arrival of this report, there were three outstanding leaders that developed, PayPal, Liberty Reserve and E-gold, which by chance was started by Nick Szabo, a previous DigiCash worker and e-contract trailblazer.

While PayPal was mindful to arrange and maintain a strategic distance from the difficulties caused by creating a digital currency directly, the other two in the long run ran afoul of officials in the US because of the way they were used for illegal activities. These three, early e-money frameworks, essentially worked as centralized frameworks, marking a clear difference from the decentralized cryptocurrencies that would soon arrive on the scene.

Cryptocurrencies: The dawn of the modern cryptocurrency can be traced back to 2009 when a number of programmers in a peer-to-peer programming forum were discussing the benefits of a successful digital currency that maintained the best aspects of physical cash with none of its restrictions. While most of the people who were part of the discussion were simply speculating, there was one user, a person or group of people using the alias Satoshi Nakamoto, who was doing far more than that. Soon after this fateful discussion, Nakamoto returned to the message board with the opensource code for blockchain technology, more specifically the Bitcoin blockchain, as well as a treatise on what they felt Bitcoin should be.

Shortly thereafter, Nakamoto sent bitcoins to several individuals, and minded the resulting transaction, and Bitcoin was off and running. Sometime after the initial round of bitcoins was dispersed, one individual traded 10,000 bitcoins in exchange for a two large pizzas worth about $20, placing the initial value of each bitcoin at around $.002. For reference, one bitcoin is currently worth about $17,000.

At this point, interest in the future of the novel new type of currency was coming in from developers at all sides. Confident that their creation was in good hands, the Nakamoto alias soon faded into the background, never to be heard from again after early 2010. However, rumor has it that somewhere out there is a bitcoin wallet with more than a billion dollars' worth of bitcoin at current prices.

While the early years were largely marked by slow growth and darknet transactions, by 2014 the price of bitcoin was starting to rise to the point that investors started to take notice. This was also the year that marked the first time a cryptocurrency hit $1,000. While there have been some serious swings since that time, the price of bitcoins has overall continued to only increase.

Ethereum

As of the end of 2017, Ethereum is the second biggest name in cryptocurrency, but likely the largest name when it comes to promoting blockchain technology. The primary cryptocurrency it is based on a technology known as ether, though it can primarily be thought of as a development platform for developers looking to create their own cryptocurrencies or their own applications that take advantage of blockchain technology. Ether is typically used as a way to pay for services and any relevant transactions that are made through the applications that are designed to run on the platform. In addition to this, ether sees a fair amount of speculative investment with one ether being worth about $450 at the end of 2017.

First created by a man named Vitalik Buterin, in 2015, Ethereum's other biggest asset is the fact that it was built from the ground up with smart contracts in mind, which allows for a far greater variety of functionality than what the smart contracts that run on the Bitcoin blockchain are capable of. This is due in large part to the fact that Buterin started out as a developer at Bitcoin before authoring a white paper about a programing language for Bitcoin in 2013. His idea was turned down, but instead of giving up, he quit his job and spent 2014 building a blockchain from the ground up. The result is the Ethereum platform, which has the stated goal of actively working to make traditional contract services straightforward, and therefore as cheap as possible.

While Bitcoin got to where it is today by being the first out of the gate, Ethereum has slowly but surely been gaining popularity in both the consumer and professional levels thanks to the high quality way that its functionality is implemented and the fact that it easily allows businesses to utilize smart contracts in ways never before imagined. The potential here has already attracted interest from some serious names, so much so that in early 2017 more than 30 corporations, developers and non-profit organizations came together to form what is known as the Ethereum Enterprise Alliance. Membership has already grown to more than 100 organizations including the likes of Intel, JP Morgan and Microsoft.

The stated goal of the Alliance is to work to create blockchain protocols that will offer a standard for businesses all around the world to adopt to ensure that everyone is on the same page. This blockchain will be specifically tailored to meet the needs of business enterprises. The idea is for the business sector to get behind the new technology in a big way and propel the technology into the mainstream as a result.

Besides the heavyweight support it has already received, Ethereum also has numerous other things going for it that make it likely that it is going to stick around in the long-term. First and foremost is the fact that it runs on a blockchain 2.0 variation, which means it naturally has several advantages when compared to Bitcoin. Additionally, it is able to scale more easily to accommodate a far greater number of simultaneous users than Bitcoin. This remains the case despite the fact that a majority of the blocks in the Ethereum blockchain contain more data than Bitcoin blocks, because many of them include smart contracts as well. These benefits are already being taken advantage of by both programmers and consumers, both of which are moving to Ethereum in record numbers. This is not just an idle hyperbole either, the Ethereum platform has already processed about half as many transactions as Bitcoin, despite only being active a little more than two years.

The decentralized apps (DApp) that are made possible on the Ethereum blockchain are able to run based on tokens which the creator of the DApp can create as well. These tokens can then be used to form new cryptocurrencies, or to represent abstract concepts such as proofs of membership or virtual shares in a company. These tokens are then generally compatible with the standard Ethereum APIs as well as most Ethereum wallets. The expression "token" may imply many things: a token can be utilized to give clients access to a (de)centralized computer application that serves as a key for the execution of digital transactions or stand as a unit of currency (e.g. bitcoins).

DApp tokens must be produced and circulated by a standard algorithm or set of criteria. Tokens constitute the reason for utilizing an application, and are additionally a reward for commitments by clients. However, tokens do not serve any benefits, nor do they offer rights to profits or value shares. Although, the worth of a DApp token may go up or decline after some time, it would be a misinterpretation to consider them a sort of security.

What Systems are Utilized to Disseminate Tokens?

There are three general mechanism DApps (e.g. Bitcoin, Ethereum) which can be utilized in disseminating their tokens (e.g. bitcoins, ether).

They are as follows:

- **Mining:** tokens are conveyed as a reward to those members who unravel certain confirmation operations most rapidly (with agreement being built up by proof of work). Bitcoin is one case of a DApp issuing its tokens through mining.

- **Fundraising:** tokens are appropriated to the individuals who financed the initial designing of the DApp.
- **Development:** tokens are produced utilizing a predefined system and are accessible for the future development of the DApp (with agreement being set up by proof of stake).

When tokens are created in great enough numbers, they can be used as a means for new companies to crowdfund startup capital outside of more standardized channels. Once the tokens have been created, the crowdfunding process can be linked to smart contracts, which can, in turn, be set to only transfer all of the funds to the company's account if certain goals are obtained.

Bitcoin vs Ethereum

When comparing the two biggest names in the cryptocurrency space, the biggest difference that you are going to find is the focus of the blockchain. Bitcoin is exclusively concerned with offering digital, cryptocurrency transactions while Ethereum is all about pushing its platform as a space for blockchain development, smart contract utilization and decentralized application use.

Rate at which new blocks are created: The Bitcoin blockchain is only able to create a new block every 10 minutes in order to remain operating at peak efficiency. As it is built on a much more recent foundation, the Ethereum platform, on the other hand, is able to generate a new block in just 12 seconds using a proprietary ghost protocol. This is not without its downsides, however, as the ghost protocol also makes it easier for blocks to stall during the verification process, especially during periods of extreme stress on the network.

Number of Units Available

As of the end of 2017, only about 30 percent of all the bitcoins that will ever be generated remain unaccounted for. As there are a fixed number of Bitcoins out there, the last is estimated to be mined around 2140, this means that if you are just getting into Bitcoin, today, it is significantly more difficult to get a hold of a bitcoin than it was just two years ago. A vast majority of all the available Bitcoins were mined during the early days of the service, everything after that has just been a clean up mission. On the other hand, only about 40 percent of all the potential ether out there has been mined which means there is still time to get in before the market gets too crowded to make it easy to remain competitive.

As previously mentioned, there is already an end date estimated for Bitcoin, at least in its current form. This is due to the fact that the amount that is rewarded to miners for verifying bitcoins is calculated in such a way that it naturally cuts itself in half each time a specific number of blocks are mined. Currently the reward for mining a bitcoin transaction is 12 bitcoins (split among everyone who contributed to the task), but the reward decrease to just 6 bitcoins is estimated to take place in 2022. Meanwhile, Ethereum was created to ensure that the amount of verification reward remains at a standard 5 ether, as long as the proof of work model remains in action.

Fees

The fees that users pay to complete transactions on each of the major blockchains varies as well. Bitcoin charges a flat rate, regardless of the size or complexity of the transaction. While this is good for those who regularly complete large, complex, transactions, for most people it is going to end up being cheaper to complete a transaction on the Ethereum platform.

When completing a transaction on the Ethereum platform, the platform treats transactions of different sizes in different ways. The Ethereum payment system is known as gas and the amount of gas that a specific transaction is going to require is going to depend on a combination of three things. First, the amount of storage that the transaction is going to require. Next, the complexity of the transaction overall and finally, the bandwidth that is going to be used as a result of adding the transaction to the blockchain. The total cost that the transaction will cost to complete will then be shown as both its gas price and gas limit.

If you compare an Ethereum transaction to buying gasoline for your vehicle, then the gas limit is the number of gallons of gasoline that your car will hold and the gas price is the price per gallon. This is written as x amount of GWEI (price) per gas (unit). To fill up your "tank", it takes... - 10 gallons at $2.50 = $25 - 21000 units of gas at 20 GWEI = 0.00042 ETH. Therefore, the total TX fee will be 0.00042 Ether. Sending tokens will typically take ~50000 gas to ~100000 gas, so the total TX fee increases to 0.001 ETH - 0.002 ETH.

For an Ethereum transaction, the gas limit can be thought of as the maximum amount you can pay for the transaction in question, based on its gas price. Knowing this amount is crucial, especially if you are dealing with a DApp as it can easily prevent you from spending 1 ether instead of .01 ether all at once. Regardless, you will need to keep in mind that the units of gas that will be required for a specified transaction is going to be defined by the precise way the code is executed in the blockchain. This means that if you want to decrease the amount of gas that you will spend on a transaction, you will need to focus on making the transaction less complex, not decreasing its overall gas limit.

If you do not have the fees to complete a transaction successfully, you will receive an error notifying you that you are out of gas. On the other hand, if you end up overfunding a transaction the leftover gas will be added back to your account after the fact. Overall, you can spend as much as 21,000 gas on a single transaction.

During non-peak transaction hours, 40GWEI will be enough to get your transaction into the very next block that is verified, while 20 GWEI will be enough to see your transaction is verified within five blocks and 2 GWEI will get your transaction processed within no more than two minutes.

When you go ahead and pay to have a transaction processed properly, those on the Ethereum platform will process much faster than those on the Bitcoin blockchain due to what is known as the Turning Complete Code. This code ensures that the Ethereum platform can complete virtually any calculation as long as it has all the time it needs to do so. While it ensures transactions process more quickly, it also leaves the Ethereum platform open to additional forms of attack, including a summer 2017 attack that was so serious it caused a permanent fork in the Ethereum platform's blockchain.

Usage Pattern

Blockchains, and cryptocurrencies, are naturally social constructs. This means that the more people who use them, the more useful they become, which in turn generates another round of increased usage and so on and so forth. Ethereum is already proving more effective in this capacity as well, as Bitcoin has already reached the maximum number of transactions it can handle in a day. In fact, it currently has a backlog that would take nearly a week to clear up properly. Meanwhile, the Ethereum blockchain is nowhere near its limit and the creation of the Ethereum Enterprise Alliance, not to mention the Alliance's goals, indicates that its social currency is only likely to increase in the near future.

Chapter 7: Blockchain in the Future

What Is Covered In This Chapter?

The Future that Blockchain Holds
How it Will Shape the Economy

While Bitcoin and Ethereum are both finally reaching a size where they can start to somewhat stabilize the cryptocurrency market, the shear number of cryptocurrencies in this space means that it is still going to be quite some time before things settle down. The blockchain market as a whole is much the same with countless different startup companies out there looking to carve out a piece of the niche for themselves while there is still time to do so. When you take all of this volatility, and combine it with what is taking place with the Ethereum Alliance and in various other places throughout the corporate space, it can be easy to give up the future of blockchain as impossible to predict because there are too many variables to track. This is not quite accurate, as long as you content yourself with the big picture you will come to realize that blockchain holds a strong position for the future.

Policy & Regulation

Like many new technologies, both cryptocurrency and blockchain technology have gone from overnight successes, to codified industries before government regulation had the time to catch up. This does not mean that they are not going to regulate, rather that regulation is likely coming sooner rather than later. This process was set in motion when the first Bitcoin holders almost immediately went out and started using their anonymous cryptocurrency to start buying all sorts of illegal things on the Silk Road Marketplace. Now that Bitcoins have reached $17,000 per unit, they are no longer on the fringe, they are big business, and you can bet that governments around the world are considering the best ways in which to handle what could be a serious issue if left unchecked.

Already, numerous US government agencies including the Department of Homeland Security (DHS), the Federal Bureau of Investigation (FBI) and the Securities and Exchange Commission (SEC) are all looking for ways to ensure that cryptocurrency, and blockchain technology as a result, are regulated in such a way that they will not actively promote crime. This increasing level of scrutiny first started coming to the fore in 2013 when a federal ruling came down declaring that cryptocurrency exchanges were operating as a money service business which meant that they were inherently subject to the same laws as other businesses of that type. This, in turn, allowed DHS to step in and freeze the account of the largest Bitcoin exchange at the time, Mt. Gox, amid charges of money laundering.

This incident can then be directly linked to a 2017 SEC ruling that denied Bitcoin the right to create an official Bitcoin exchange traded fund. This ruling cost Bitcoin about a fourth of its unit price overall, though it did little to hurt its extreme growth during much of 2017. The SEC was still reviewing this decision at the end of 2017.

This decision has left Bitcoin in somewhat of a lurch, and one that will affect cryptocurrency and blockchain technology as a result. The increased popularity and usage cases means that cryptocurrency is more popular than ever, but this popularity has lead to a demand for regulation of the sort that Bitcoin was specifically created to rally against in the first place. Likewise, while there are more and more users taking advantage of the Bitcoin blockchain for the first time every day, there are still not yet enough of them, nor are they vocal enough, to demand that the government back off and allow the current status quo to remain. These issues need to be resolved before a mass saturation point is reached, otherwise, it is unlikely it ever will be to anyone's satisfaction.

In order to ensure that it has an eventual place in the financial system, programmers will need to find a way to allow it to remain true to the vision Nakamoto expressed in his treatise, while still giving concessions when it comes to the ease with which the current system can be corrupted in the name of illegal activity. Furthermore, all this needs to occur without decreasing its current level of security or making the blockchain more difficult to access. Needless to say, future cryptocurrencies could easily end up being more of an amalgamation of the current definition and more traditional fiat currencies.

As all cryptocurrencies run on blockchain, three of the world's superpowers using blockchain on a national level will represent the biggest use of the technology by far and will cement it as more than a passing fad in the minds of many. The US, Russia and China are all looking into this revolutionary technology.

Fedcoin: One way that the future of cryptocurrency could go could be that of a government-controlled cryptocurrency that essentially serves as the digital version of the traditional fiat currency, like the original digital currency but based around blockchain technology. There  is currently reason to believe that the Federal Reserve is actively working out the logistics surrounding the creation of a national cryptocurrency that would be directly connected to the dollar.

This is largely based on a 2016 meeting that was attended by banking bigwigs from around the world, cryptocurrency aficionados and Bitcoin higher ups and was overseen by the chairman of the Federal Reserve herself. This potential cryptocurrency is tentatively being called Fedcoin and it would run on a fork of the Bitcoin blockchain. From a technical perspective, getting it up and running would be as easy as forking the Bitcoin blockchain, generating a new genesis block and having a system in place to ensure verification worked properly. The biggest difference between Fedcoin and Bitcoin, then, would be the fact that while Bitcoin is public and decentralized, Fedcoin would be centralized which means that the Federal Reserve would be able to view every transaction and veto those it does not like.

Logistically, to get the system up and running, all that would need to be done would be to offer people an exchange rate of 1 to 1 between Fedcoin and the dollar. As Fedcoin would also be easier to track than traditional fiat currencies, it is likely that, over time, physical currencies would become more and more difficult to find. All told, the goal of the Federal Reserve appears to be the stabilization of the cryptocurrency market through a direct connection to a fiat currency. It does not seem terribly interested in ensuring that the link is voluntary either, as long as it is unbreakable.

Russia's bid to stabilize its economy: In early 2017, the Russian government reversed a previous decry stating that anyone using cryptocurrency could be sentenced to jail time. While, superficially, this reversal appeared to come out of nowhere, it is actually the latest attempt by the country to prevent a total collapse of their economy. To understand why this is the case, it is important to keep in mind that for the past several years Russia's economy has been in a bad way thanks to decreasing oil prices and a wide variety of economic sanctions that make it difficult for the country to find outside investors.

All told, this has led to serious issues within the banking sector, when it comes to accessing money and several large-scale schemes have been uncovered to remove large amounts of capital from the country. In striving to fight this problem, the national banking system has already shut down more than 100 banks of various sizes throughout the country and plans to close at least that many more before things are said and done. Closing banks is not cheap, apparently, and this process has already cost the country more than $50 billion. Furthermore, it has also created serious concerns for the country when it comes to its overall level of liquidity.

With the correct framing, it then becomes clear that this reversal on the idea of cryptocurrency might not represent a change of heart at the highest levels, it could instead simply be a means of providing Russian citizens with as many different currency options as possible to ensure that the problem is not magnified by people trying, and failing, to get their money out of traditional financial institutions. Likewise, there is hope that an increased focus on cryptocurrency will help the country move away from its relationship-based banking model that leaves smaller private banks operating essentially autonomously and completely outside the regulatory control of the state.

As of the end of 2017, Russia does not appear to be interested in creating its own unique cryptocurrency, along the lines of Fedcoin, and instead seems more interested in a loosely connected national decentralized ledger that will give them the ability to track individual transactions, without forcing to go through the trouble of creating and tracking an entire new currency, something it certainly cannot afford at the moment. Likewise, the means that the country will take when it comes to bringing their digital ledger remains a mystery as they could already be working on their own, though it would be far faster to fork an existing blockchain instead. In all likelihood, they will start with an existing blockchain to test the efficacy of the system before moving to something specially created down the line, when the current round of crises have passed.

Finally, it is important to keep in mind that the decree that cryptocurrency usage is no longer illegal came through traditional government channels, it is unclear just where support for cryptocurrency is coming from. This is especially important in Russia where a plan that is supported by the highest levels of government is far more likely to ever see the light of day than something supported only by the national bank.

First Official Announcement

While other world powers are still mulling over how they want to roll out their national blockchains, China has already announced the successful completion of testing of its own centralized blockchain, along with the first national cryptocurrency by completing transactions between the People's Bank and other, local and commercial banks. While not much else is currently known about the cryptocurrency, it is believed that it is able to scale almost infinitely, based on the number of transactions taking place at a given point and time. Furthermore, its release is anticipated to coincide with the rollout of the renminbi, which will be a huge step forwards towards legitimizing both blockchain and cryptocurrency at the highest levels.

This rollout goes to show just how committed to the idea of cryptocurrency China is, regardless of the economic, technical and logistical challenges that may arise as a result. While there is no way to guess how things will work out for this new blockchain and cryptocurrency in the long-term, it is undeniably going to have serious ramifications on the world stage, in one way or another.

The most important fact to keep in mind here is that this will mark the first digital fiat currency which means that the physical and digital version will naturally retain parity with one another. This, in turn, will significantly alter the way that a wide variety of financial transactions take place, virtually overnight. This is due to the fact that having access to the cryptocurrency form of the currency will mark the first time that more than 10 million Chinese citizens will have access to any form of traditional banking services. The additional impact of this many people having access to only services at the same time is going to be substantial.

Besides providing access to services that have literally never before been available, the blockchain of the cryptocurrency will also give the government a much more detailed look at the transactions its citizens are making, giving policymakers a much more granular view of the economy than what was previously available. It will also help the country to crackdown on corruption in the financial sector. Finally, it will go a long way towards giving the government some form of control over cryptocurrency trading, something that it is very anxious to gain as Chinese investors have become very involved in international cryptocurrency investment in the past decade.

Launching the new cryptocurrency at the same time as the renminbi will also go a long way towards ensuring that this new currency catches on as well, not just locally but worldwide. The fact that buyers anywhere in the world will be able to purchase the currency through a blockchain, without having to go through traditional money exchange procedures, means that it is likely most people will avoid the traditional path, and many may likely purchase renminbi instead of other types of cryptocurrency as a result. It will also mark the first time that a cryptocurrency can be purchased directly, without the need for a traditional cryptocurrency exchange. Once it hits the market, cryptocurrency as a whole will be validated in a way that will make even the most diehard skeptics sit up and take notice.

Conclusion

Thank you for making it through to the end of *Blockchain: A Complete Guide to Understanding Blockchain*, I hope it was informative and able to provide you with all of the tools you need to understand what blockchain is.

When it comes to blockchain technology, it is important to keep in mind that the technology is still so new that there could be major changes to the existing paradigm. As such, it is important to keep in mind that what you have learned here is just an introduction, in order to truly remain informed on blockchain technology you are going to need to keep updating current information.

Likewise, it is important to keep in mind that while there is currently plenty of speculative interest around both blockchain and cryptocurrency, the potentially life changing investment deals that it represents is not going to stick around forever and every day you wait is a day that is potentially costing you money. While you certainly have the time to carefully consider the options ahead of you, this will not remain the case forever which is why it is better to get with the program sooner rather than later if at all possible. Strike while the iron is hot, and you will find yourself better off because of it.

Finally, if you found this book useful in any way, a review is always appreciated!

You May Also Enjoy the Following Titles from Cryptomasher

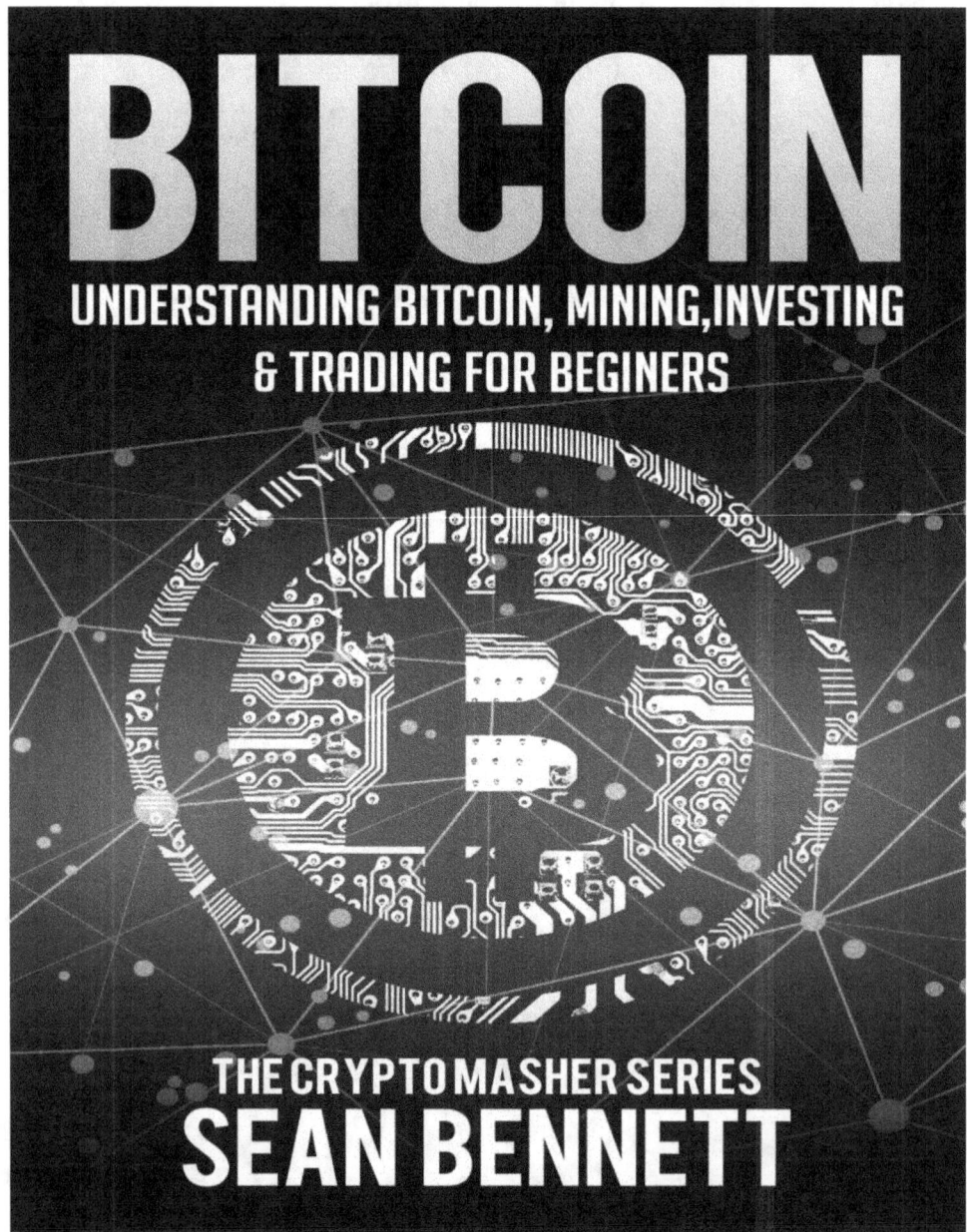

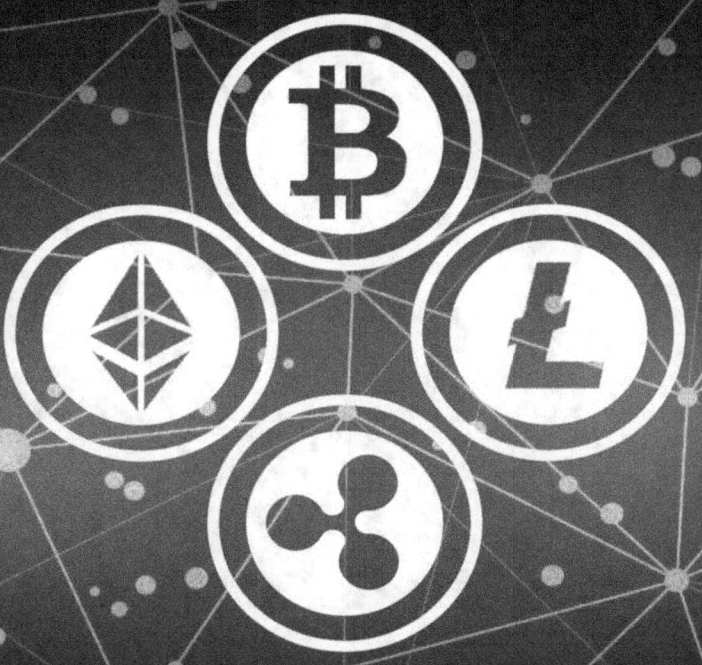

CRYPTOCURRENCY

UNDERSTANDING BITCOIN, BITCOIN CASH, ETHEREUM & ALTCOINS

THE CRYPTO MASHER SERIES
SEAN BENNETT

FREE eBook Available
This is my FREE GIFT to YOU

Click on the link below to collect your
FREE GIFT & Avoid the 5 Deadly
Mistakes

http://eepurl.com/c9Lsr9